My Mother

Thomas Campbell

Dedication

I would like to dedicate this book
to all my teachers and volunteers
(Ruth Sedgwick, Karen Hulston, Karen Aiello,
Jan Goulding, Ben Zwierink, Jean Wright,
Jeff Billington and Jill Fernando)
and the Home Tuition Project.

Teachers and volunteers
don't get rewarded
but they make a big difference
to the lives of ordinary people.
Thanks also to Steph and Anne
for giving me the chance
to publish this story.

I can remember bits and pieces
about my mother.
She used to tell me about her father.
He was a very cruel man.

She married my father
to get away from her own family.
I think she really walked
into the lion's mouth.

He was a very,
very violent man,
worse than her own father.
If he was alive now
he would kill me for saying this.

I remember one night
he threatened me
in a pub.
My family were sat
around the table.

We were talking
about my mother.
She wasn't there.
She had been dead
for three months at this time.

My father had a fierce habit
of calling us all bastards.
He said to us,
"How do you know
that your mother didn't have any bastards?"

I said,
"The only bastard that my mother had
was the day she put the ring on you!"

Then he went for me across the table.

I wasn't frightened.

I was delighted.

I was telling him the truth.

The truth hurt him.

The whole family had to pull him off me.
His very words were,
“If I had a shotgun, I would shoot you”.

My mother often told me
that her father wanted
to keep her away from my father.
He knew the type of man he was.

The morning of her wedding
her father said,
"Now, Kate, you're going out to get married
but you will rue the day
you put that ring on".

She couldn't look at another man.

My father was the fierce jealous type.

One night she tried to escape from a window.

He dragged her back in by her hair.

Another night he came back from the pub.

He kicked her with a steel-capped boot.

I saw it all.

I couldn't do anything about it.

The only time she cried
was when she had a drink.

I often sat at the side of her bed
and she told me stories from her past.
I didn't know what to do
when she started to cry.
She had a very sad life.

About the Author

I only started school aged nine,
because I was epileptic.
The school was a boarding school in Ireland,
run by the Sisters of Charity.
They said I was brain damaged
and I would never be able to read or write.

I left school at sixteen
still not able to read or write.
Years later I settled in England.
I bought a computer.
I thought it would help me
to read and write.

I didn't know about computers
so I went to a computer class.
My teacher was also an English teacher.
Later I had a new teacher, Jan.
She helped me overcome my dyslexia.

I also have two volunteer tutors.
One helps me with computers.
The other helps me with English.
Now I feel more confident.
I hope that you enjoy reading this story.
If you have problems like mine,
you can get help from volunteers.

Thomas Campbell

What is New Leaf?

New Leaf is a brand new and unique community publishing project set up to publish and promote writing by ordinary people who would normally never expect to see their own words in print. We aim to develop adults' reading and writing skills using creative reading and writing activities and by publishing writings by and for adults who are working to improve their reading and writing skills.

Although we are new, we are not wet behind the ears! The project has been set up by two dedicated and experienced community publishers who have both worked in this field for many years for different organisations which have now sadly disappeared. We were determined that tried and tested methods and principles which have proved so successful many times over must not be lost. We see ourselves as the true descendants of a proud tradition which has been established over the last thirty years and which we will carry forward to a brighter future!

Booklist available

New Leaf Readers
5, Cranleigh Close
Walton
Warrington
WA4 6SD
Tel: 07984 241 863
E-mail: amchester@btinternet.com
www.newleafpublishing.org.uk